648
TAN

Washing

Gill Tanner and Tim Wood

2 13

Photographs by Maggie Murray

Illustrations by Mark Peppé

A & C Black · London

Here are some of the people you will meet in this book.

The Miller Family in 1990

The Grant Family in 1960

Tony Miller is the same age as you.
His sister, Jane, is eight years old.
What is Tony's mum called?

This is Tony's mum, Helen,
when she was nine years old, in 1960.
She is with her mum and dad,
her brother and her baby sister.

The Brown Family in 1930

Victoria Brown
Robert Brown
Emma
Rose and John

The Jennings Family in 1900

Thomas Jennings
Anna Jennings
Joe
Sam
Mary
Victoria
Edward

This is Tony's granny, Rose,
when she was just a baby, in 1930.
Her brother, John, is looking after her.

This is Tony's great grandma, Victoria,
when she was six years old, in 1900.
Can you see what her brothers and
her sister are called?

How many differences can you spot between these two pictures?

One shows washday in a modern house and one shows washday in a house one hundred years ago.

This book is about washing clothes.

It will help you find out how washday has changed in the last hundred years.

There are twelve mystery objects in this book and you can find out what they are.
They will tell you a lot about people in the past.

The Jennings family used this on washday one hundred years ago.

The wooden part was a bit wider than a person's shoulders.

It was used to carry something.

Can you guess what it was for?

Turn the page to find out.

Can you find the mystery object in this picture?
It's a **yoke**.
Sam filled buckets with water from the pump outside.
He used the yoke to carry the buckets to the wash house.

Mary emptied the buckets into the copper
while Anna lit the fire to heat the water.
In those days, not many people had an inside tap.
All the water which the Jennings family needed
for washing had to be collected from the pump
and heated in the copper.

Anna Jennings often used these three things together.
They helped her to get the dirty clothes clean.

Turn the page to find out what they are.

Can you spot the mystery objects?
They are a **washboard**, a **scrubbing brush**
and a **bar of soap**.

In those days people couldn't buy washing powder.
Dirty clothes were boiled in the copper.
Then collars and cuffs were rubbed with soap
and scrubbed on the washboard with the brush.

The clothes in those days
were mainly made from cotton, wool or linen.
What are your clothes made of?

This mystery object is a bit taller
than a chair.
Look very closely.
See if you can guess how it worked.
Anna used it so that she did not have to
put her hands into the hot water.
Turn the page to find out what it is.

The mystery object is called a **dolly peg**.

Anna Jennings filled the dolly tub with water and put in the clothes.

She grated some soap into the water.
Then she twisted the handle of the dolly peg backwards and forwards to wash the clothes.
The short legs of the dolly peg
churned the dirty clothes around in the water.
Then Anna rinsed the clothes in clean water.

These mystery objects belonged to Victoria Brown in 1930.

You can guess what the bigger one is for.

But what are the two smaller ones?

Victoria Brown used them when she was rinsing the clothes.

Turn the page to find out what they are.

This is Victoria Brown's washday in 1930.
How is it different from her mother's washday?
Where did her water come from?
Can you see the mystery objects?
They are a box of **soap flakes**
and two **'blue' bags**.

Emma put the soap flakes into the
washing machine.
Then she turned the handle to make
the dolly stick inside turn round.

Victoria rinsed out the white clothes.
She squeezed a 'blue' bag
into the rinsing water.

The 'blue bag' turned the water blue,
and made the clothes whiter.

This mystery object is nearly as tall as you are.

Victoria Brown used it before she hung the washing out to dry.

What happened when she turned the handle?

What do you think this object was for?

Turn the page to find out.

The mystery object is a **mangle**.

John turned the handle round and round.
Victoria Brown folded the wet sheets carefully
and guided them through the rollers of the mangle.
As the rollers turned they squeezed the water
out of the sheets.

Emma folded the sheets neatly into a basket
and then hung them on the washing line.
When the mangle was not being used,
the flat top was swung up to make it into a useful table.

You can probably guess one of these mystery objects.

It gets too hot to touch.
In your home you have something like this which works from electricity.
But do you know what makes this one hot?
What is the other object?

Turn the page to find out.

Can you spot the mystery objects?
They are a **gas iron** and its **stand**.
The gas came along a pipe from a tap on the wall.
Victoria Brown used a match to light
the gas jets inside the iron.

She did not find her gas iron easy to use.
Sometimes the flames blew out.
Sometimes they burned the clothes.
So Victoria saved up to buy an electric iron instead.

Rose Grant used this mystery object on washdays in 1960.
It did two important jobs and made washing much easier.
Can you guess what it is?

Turn the page to find out.

This is washday in the Grants' kitchen in 1960.

How is it different from washday in the Browns' kitchen?

Rose Grant is having a coffee with her neighbour.

The mystery object is a **'twin-tub' washing machine**.

The tub on the left washed the clothes.

The tub on the right spun them dry.

The machine worked by electricity.

When the washing and drying were finished
the washing machine pumped the dirty water into the sink.

These mystery objects were used together.
You may have some things like them in your home.
Can you guess how these objects
were used on washday?
Can you work out how they fitted together?

Turn the page to find the answers.

Can you spot the mystery objects?
Two of the objects unfold and become **hangers**.
The other one is a **plastic bar with a sucker** on the end.

The sucker fixes the bar to the wall
so it can hold the hangers.

Peter hung his shirts
on the hangers to drip dry.

His shirts were made of nylon,
which was a new material in those days.
The nylon shirts dried without any creases
so he didn't have to iron them.

Now that you know a bit more about washday
and how it has changed
over the last one hundred years,
see if you can guess
what these mystery objects are.

They are made of wood.
Their shape should give you a big clue.
What are they?

You will find the answer on page 24.

Time-line

These pages show you the objects in this book and the objects we use for washing nowadays.

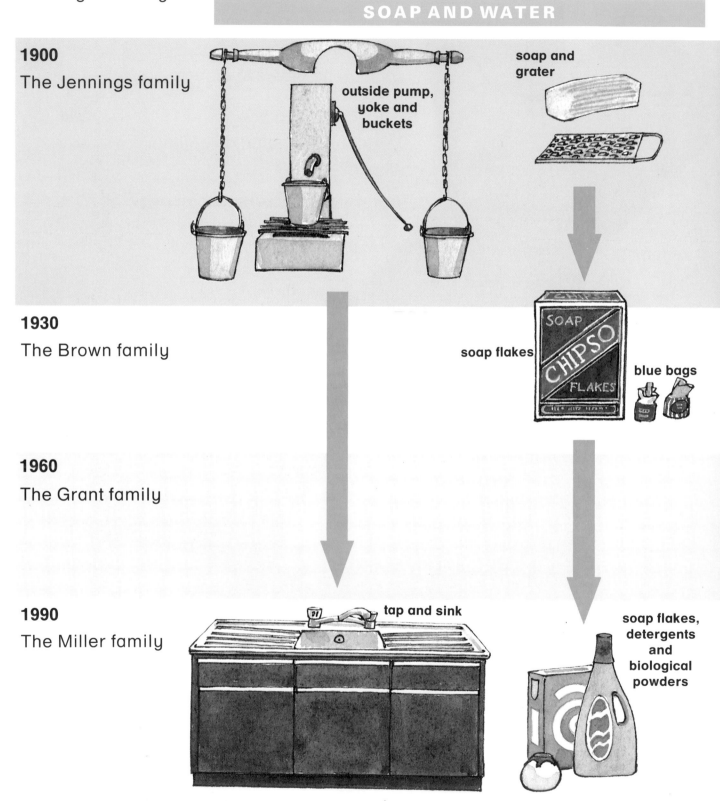

SOAP AND WATER

1900
The Jennings family

outside pump, yoke and buckets

soap and grater

1930
The Brown family

soap flakes

CHIPSO SOAP FLAKES

blue bags

1960
The Grant family

1990
The Miller family

tap and sink

soap flakes, detergents and biological powders

WASHING AND DRYING

IRONING

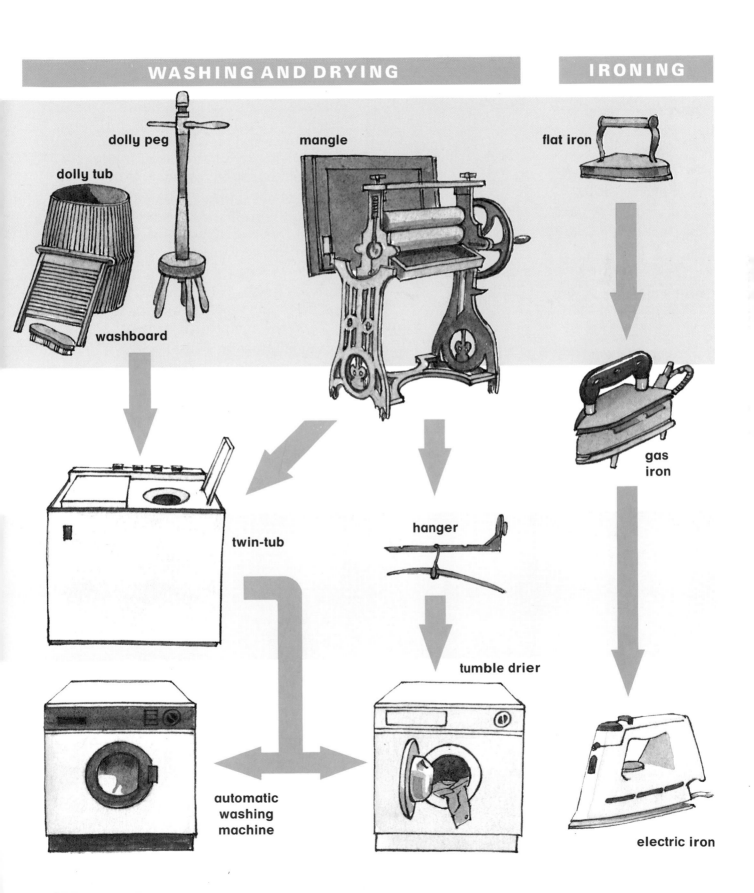

dolly peg

dolly tub

mangle

flat iron

washboard

twin-tub

gas iron

hanger

tumble drier

automatic washing machine

electric iron

Index

The **mystery objects** on page 21 were **wooden legs**, used when Victoria Jennings was a child. Woollen stockings were pulled over the legs so that they dried in the right shape without wrinkles.

For parents and teachers

More about the objects and pictures in this book

Pages 5/6   The Jennings family lived in a large industrial town. In 1900, only very rich people had piped water. Most people carried water from the nearest pump or tap to a wash house in the back yard.

Pages 7/8   Washing clothes 100 years ago usually took a whole day. Early washboards were made of wood. Later ones had harder-wearing metal ridges.

Pages 9/10   The dolly tub and dolly peg were the first 'washing machine'. The tub was filled and emptied by hand.

Pages 11/12   The Browns lived in a semi-detached house in a small town. The washing was done in the kitchen. Note the running water and electric light. The first soap powder was invented in the U.S.A. in 1843. The first detergent (Persil) was made in 1907.

Pages 13/14   Three people were needed to work the mangle, and a vast amount of water spilled on the floor. The first electric spin-driers did not reach Britain until 1956.

Pages 15/16   The Victorians used irons heated on the kitchen range or filled with hot coals. The electric iron was introduced to Britain in 1892, but few homes had electricity. Other models included irons filled with petrol.

Pages 17/18   The Grants lived in one of the new towns built in the 1960s. Twin-tubs were electric but not automatic. They had to be filled with a hose, and wet clothes had to be moved from the washing tub to the spinner. The introduction of these machines ended the need for a 'washday'.

Pages 19/20   Plastics suitable for making household objects were not developed until the 1930s. They were widely used in homes during the 1950s. The increased use of synthetic fibres in the 1960s led to more drip-dry garments coming on to the market.

Things to do

History Mysteries will provide an excellent starting point for all kinds of history work. There are a lot of general ideas which can be drawn out of the pictures, particularly in relation to the way houses, clothes, family size and lifestyles have changed in the last 100 years. Below are some starting points and ideas for follow up activities:

1   Work on families and family trees can be developed from the family on pages 2/3, bearing in mind that many children do not come from two-parent nuclear families. Why do the people in the book have different surnames even though they are related? How have their clothes and hair styles changed over time?

2   Find out more about washing in the past, from a variety of sources including interviews with older people in the community, magazines, books and manufacturers' information. Washday wasn't the same for everyone. Why not?

3   There is one object which is in the pictures of the 1900s, 1930s and 1960s washday. Can you find it?

4   Experiment to find the most effective ways to wash clothes, using a variety of fabrics and equipment.

5   Look at the difference between the photographs and the illustrations in this book. What different kinds of things can they tell you?

6   Make your own collection of clothes, and washing objects or pictures. You can build up an archive or school museum over several years by encouraging children to bring in old objects, collecting unwanted items from parents, collecting from junk shops and jumble sales. You may also be able to borrow handling collections from your local museum or library service.

7   Encouraging the children to look at the objects is a useful start, but they will get more out of this if you organise some practical activities which help to develop their powers of observation. These might include drawing the objects, describing an object to another child who must then pick out the object from the collection, or writing descriptions of the objects for labels or catalogue cards.

8   Encourage the children to answer questions. What do the objects look and feel like? What are they made of? What were they used for? Who made them? What makes them work? How old are they? How could you find out more about them? Do they do the jobs they are supposed to do?

9   What do the objects tell us about the people who used them? Children might do some writing, drawing or role play, imagining themselves as the owners of different objects.

10   Children might find a mystery object in their own home for the others to draw, write about and identify. Children can compare the objects in the book with objects in their own homes.

11   If you have an exhibition, try pairing old objects with their nearest modern counterparts. Talk about each pair. Some useful questions might be: How can you tell which is older? Which objects have changed most over time? Why? What do you think of the older objects? What would people have thought of them when they were new? Can you test how well the objects work? Is the modern version better than the older version?

12   Make a time-line using your objects. You might find the time-line at the back of this book useful. You could include pictures in your time-line and other markers to help the children gain a sense of chronology. Use your time-line to bring out the elements of *change* (eg. the gradual development of gas and electricity, the automation of the washing machine) and of *continuity* (eg. basic similarities in the processes of washing and drying, and the need for heat and water).

History Mysteries

First published 1992
A & C Black (Publishers) Limited
35 Bedford Row, London
WC1R 4JH

ISBN 0–7136–3493–6

© **1992 A & C Black (Publishers) Limited**

Reprinted 1992, 1993

A CIP catalogue record of this book is available from
The British Library.

Acknowledgements

The authors and publishers would like to thank Suella Postles and
the staff of Brewhouse Yard Museum (Nottingham),
Mrs Tanner's Tangible History,
Gordon Foulkes-Jones and the Abbey Cooker Centre
for helping to make this book possible.

Filmset by August Filmsetting, Haydock, St Helens
Printed and bound in Italy by L.E.G.O.